Between Dysynni and Dyfi

The beauty of the estuaries of the Meirionnydd coastline cannot fail to move you. Most of these rivers flow from the east to meet the waters of Bae Ceredigion in the west, where they create a rich scenic tapestry of beach and dune, against a backdrop of high mountain ridges and clear waters. Two of these rivers are Afon Dysynni and Afon Dyfi and between them lies the *ardal* (locality) of Aberdyfi and Tywyn – a hidden gem often overlooked.

The seas here have their quota of legends concerning saints and pirates, as well as fishermen's yarns still told to this day. In the mountains there are lush green *dyffrynnoedd* (river valleys) and remote *cymoedd* (pl. of *cwm*) accessible on foot, by rail or on two or four wheels.

On the shoreline and hills, traces of human habitation – whether it be an ancient fort, an old church, a ruined castle or an old boat – are a constant reminder that this *ardal* is a treasure trove of stories worth telling.

Beneath the waves

A standing stone in Dyffryn Dysynni

The Celts were warriors, travellers and great storytellers, and when they came to Wales some three thousand years ago, they left an indelible mark on the culture of this land. *Cymraeg* (the Welsh language), is a Celtic language which has preserved the nation's memory in place names, poetry and folk stories. The occasional standing stone and *cromlech* (burial chamber) in the *ardal* is further testimony to the influence of our ancestors. There are also traces of impressive Celtic hill forts, such as the one on Craig yr Aderyn near Tywyn.

The sea and mountains are an integral part of many of the old Celtic legends, as if the Other World manifests itself in morning mists and the colours of the sunset. The surf pounding the shore at Aberdyfi and Tywyn today also washes over the remains of Cantre'r Gwaelod. According to legend, Cantre'r Gwaelod was a beautiful and fertile land lying below sea level. At one time it contained towns and villages, churches and farmsteads, all protected from the waves by a system of dykes and floodgates. The man responsible for the floodgates was Seithennyn. One night, Seithennyn was too drunk to care about anything. He left the floodgates open just as a huge storm was brewing, driving the high tide before it. As a result the entire land was submerged and Cantre'r Gwaelod disappeared for ever. There are similar stories told the length and breadth of Wales as well as in the other Celtic lands, and they probably derive from a folk memory of the time when the sea levels rose at the end of the last Ice Age.

To the north of Tywyn a rocky reef known

as Sarn y Bwch stretches out to sea from the shore at the mouth of Afon Dysynni. It is said that in ancient times, Sarn y Bwch was one of the dykes which protected the lands of Cantre'r Gwaelod.

This *sarn* (causeway) is one of several similar formations which are to be seen clearly at very low tides in Bae Ceredigion – from Sarn Badrig (Patrick's causeway) near Harlech – which stretches some 35km out to sea - to Sarn Cadwgan, near Aberaeron. This, it seems, marks the territory occupied by Cantre'r Gwaelod. When the tide is exceptionally low, the roots of ancient tree trunks over 5,000 years old come into view, providing further confirmation of the old myth that at one time there was dry land where the sea is today.

There is an old Welsh folksong, *Clychau Aberdyfi*, which refers to the sound of bells (*clychau*) which can be heard rising from beneath the waves as you walk on the beach at Aberdyfi. According to the song and the legend, there were six churches in Cantre'r Gwaelod and it is the bells of these churches which are to be heard resounding in *Clychau Aberdyfi*. Another fragment of the story is that, at the beginning of the 6th century, a saint called Tudclyd had dedicated his life to the church in recompense for the misdeeds of his father. Tudclyd Sant established a church at Penmachno. And the name of his errant father? Who else but Seithennyn?

A re-created Celtic village at Castell Henllys, Penfro (Pembrokeshire)

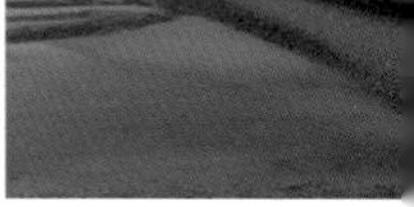

Sarn Badrig, Meirionnydd

Mynydd a llyn (Mountain and lake)

The hills around Tywyn and the Dyfi estuary rise gradually to the foot of the highest mountain in the *ardal*, Cader Idris, 878m in height. Cader Idris was once a volcano and when active was responsible for shaping the surrounding *dyffrynnoedd*.

According to legend, Idris was a giant and his *cader* (chair) was the mountain. It is hardly surprising that Idris enjoyed relaxing in this particular location, with the views from the summit of Cader Idris being particularly spectacular – better than those from the summit of Yr Wyddfa (*Snowdon*) according to many hill walkers.

Reaching its summit (Pen y Gader) in time to watch the sunset over Bae Ceredigion is a tradition among mountaineers. Another tradition is to spend the night on the mountain to watch the sun rise in the east in the morning – but you have to take care in respect of the latter. There is an old belief associated with the mountain that whoever sleeps there will either die or wake up insane or a poet.

As with all giants, Idris was well-known for his strength. At the head of Bwlch Llyn Bach (the gap above Llyn Myngul – Tal-y-llyn), in a field by the side of the road, is a boulder weighing at least twenty tonnes. This, allegedly, is a pebble which old Idris found in his shoe. While he was walking the hills one morning, he felt something irritating the sole of his foot. So he removed the offending stone and gave it a flick between finger and thumb to its present location at the head of the gap!

High in the hills to the south-east of Tywyn, there is a lake which in summer is covered with lilies and aptly known as Llyn Barfog ('the bearded lake'). It is a small circular tarn devoid of

Maen Idris

Llyn Barfog

fish. One story is that a monster used to reside at the bottom of the lake but that King Arthur dragged it out and killed it.

Another story tells how a farmer and his large family lived on the shores of Llyn Barfog. Although he worked as hard as he could all day long, the family was still very poor. One day an old woman came to the door to ask for a little food, and although things were pretty tight for the farmer and his family, his wife was willing to share what they had with the old woman. In thanking her, the old woman pledged that from that day forth there would be no more suffering on the farm.

Later that day, the farmer saw a white cow grazing with his cattle. As he milked her with the rest of the herd, he saw that her milk was much more creamy and that her daily yield was much higher than the milk the other cows could produce in a week. The milk's reputation soon spread and the farmer made a lot of money. But the old farmer was overcome by greed, and when the cow became old, he decided to fatten her and sell her to the butcher. As the butcher raised his axe to strike her down, he was suddenly paralysed. A scream rang out and a woman dressed in green was seen calling the cow and the rest of the herd home. The cattle ran from the hills into the waters of Llyn Barfog. All the farmer's newfound wealth disappeared with the herd.

Cadfan Sant and his churches

The years immediately after the Romans left the island of Britain represent a burgeoning period in the history of the *Cymry* (the Welsh people): *Oes y Seintiau* (the Age of the Saints). In other parts of the island of Britain there was considerable instability together with incursions by the barbaric tribes of the Angles and Saxons but it was a very different story here in Wales.

The sea lanes of the west were a ferment of religious and cultural links, with the *seintiau* (saints) sailing in their coracles and small craft hither and thither and establishing Christian communities in Brittany, Cornwall, Ireland, Wales, the Isle of Man and Scotland.

The Celtic Church was a monastic institution and was organised very differently from the episcopal regime of the Church of Rome. The earliest churches – the *llannau* (pl. of *llan*, lit. a piece of enclosed ground) are almost always located within reach of the sea. The *seintiau* would often establish *clasau* (schools) and associated libraries, using the indigenous languages rather than Latin. The old church in Tywyn was established by one of these early *seintiau*. Cadfan came from Llydaw (Brittany) to Tywyn to spread the Gospel in 516 AD, bringing with him a number of refugee monks. At a later date, Cadfan became the first abbot of the monastery on Enlli, the holy island which lies over the water from Tywyn at the tip of Llŷn.

It seems more than likely that the first church at Tywyn would have been a wooden construction; it was built near a well, which now lies under the foundations of a house to the north-west of the church. The memory of an old harbour nearby is preserved in the name 'Gwaliau' (sea-walls) on the road behind the

St David's statue at the Catholic church, Tywyn

church. The harbour would have served the seafaring Celtic seintiau well.

As well as prayer and scholarship, the *seintiau* were renowned for their hospitality and their medicinal skills. Gradually, Cadfan's sect expanded through the work of his disciples, maintaining Tywyn as the mother-church. However, by the Norman period, the clas at Tywyn had been developed as a secular college at Maes y Coleg, near the church, under the aegis of an abbot called Morfran. This would eventually be dissolved by Henry VIII. A large church was built there during the 12th century – the present nave is a good example of the period, with two rows of circular pillars and semi-circular arches separating them from both aisles. The old tower collapsed in 1692 and a new one was built in its place in 1736, but that was dismantled again in 1884.

There are several locations in the ardal between Dysynni and Dyfi which record the influence of Cadfan: Pistyll Cadfan ('Cadfan's waterfall'), Eisteddfa Gadfan ('Cadfan's seat') and Llwybr Cadfan ('Cadfan's path'). Aberdyfi is also part of the parish of Tywyn and its inhabitants attended the church there over the centuries. By 1837, the population of Aberdyfi had grown to such an extent that a new church was built in the village – Eglwys Pedr Sant. Ten new bells were hung in the tower to celebrate its centenary.

Maen Cadfan (Cadfan's stone)

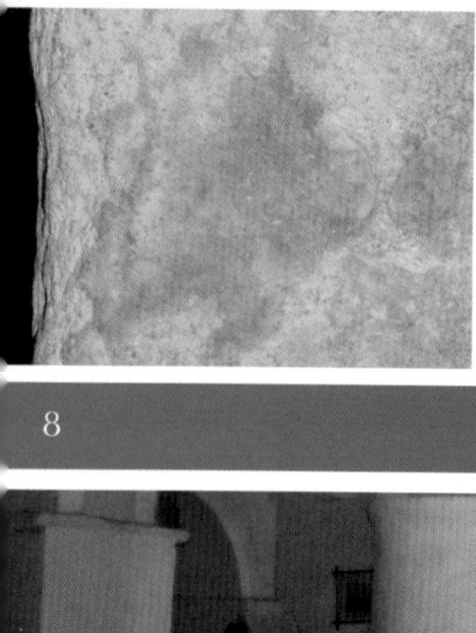

One of the most important historical relics in Wales is to be seen in the church at Tywyn – Maen Cadfan. Inscribed on the stone is, according to the experts, the oldest written example of *Cymraeg* on Welsh soil. It consists of a carved stone pillar, oblong in shape, with words inscribed on all sides.

By the 6th century, *Cymraeg* had developed as a language separate to the old Celtic Brythonic which had been spoken throughout the whole of the south of the island of Britain during the Roman occupation. Early *Cymraeg* (*Cymraeg Cynnar*) was spoken in Yr Hen Ogledd (the old north), in what is now southern Scotland, throughout northern England and the territory of modern-day Wales – making it one of Europe's oldest languages.

No complete sentence of the old Brythonic has been preserved, since Latin was the *lingua franca* at the time. Therefore, this evidence of *Cymraeg* being used in written form on Maen Cadfan in Tywyn, is very significant. Not only was *Cymraeg* a vernacular language by that time, but it was imbued with sufficient status to be used for permanent inscriptions.

Maen Cadfan was carved around the year 750 AD. Along with the epitaphs on the stone are inscribed the words CUN BEN CELEN – TRICET NITANAM ('Cun, wife of Celen – the wound remains). Even today, it is possible to see the relationship between the contemporary *Cymraeg* we use and the older form. The period of *Cymraeg Cynnar* lasted up to around 850 AD, and although there are only a few written examples, we know that a large body of literature, which was recorded at a later date in

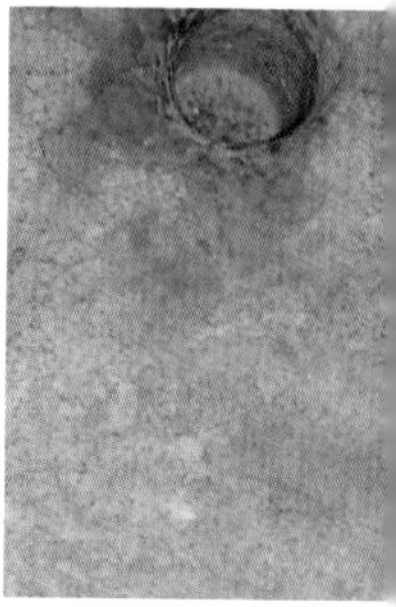

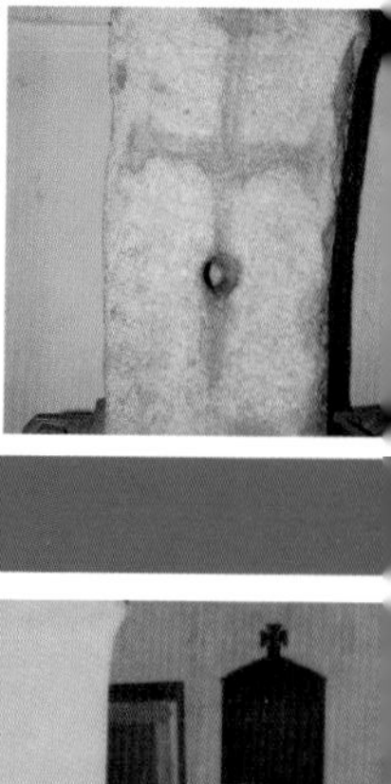

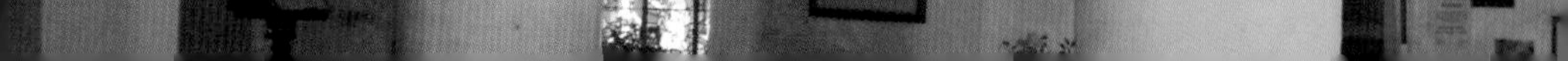

manuscripts during the Middle Ages, had been composed during those early centuries.

The poets of *Cymraeg Cynnar*, based in the various Welsh kingdoms throughout the island of Britain, wrote heroic stanzas which, as one scholar has put it, were like celebratory anthems to the birth of a new language. When Hywel Dda was king in the 10th century, the laws of Wales were codified and developed and there is no doubt that *Cymraeg* was the language of law and government at that time. The books of *Cyfraith Hywel Dda* (the law of Hywel Dda) are works of literature in their own right, such is the quality and richness of their style and vocabulary.

Maen Cadfan was carved some 200 years after the era of Cadfan Sant himself. At one time, it was believed that this memorial stone recorded the grave of the founder of the church, but, scholars have subsequently improved the interpretation of the inscription. Those named are: Celen; also Cun, the wife of Celen; Tengrui, the lawful wife of Adgan and the remains of 'three others' and 'four others' are also recorded on the stone. This is proof that prominent local families used *Cymraeg* rather than Latin even on their memorial stones. It supports all other evidence that *Cymraeg* is one of Europe's oldest literary languages.

Other old churches in the ardal

Llangelynnin

The main road running north from Tywyn in the vicinity of Llwyngwril follows the contours of the slopes between the mountains and the sea. Below the road is the 'old' church of Celynnin Sant (the new one was built in the village of Llwyngwril in 1843). The church is dedicated to a Welsh saint who was the son of Helig of Llys Helig. The ancient church is a marvellous building and it was recently restored, with due respect being paid to all its intrinsic features, the unadorned slate floor, the wooden benches and its air of simplicity. It is likely that the original building dates from 12th-13th century and was restored during the 15th century. The frescos which pre-date the Reformation have survived on the interior whitewashed walls. The graveyard faces the sea to the west and contains a number of examples of 'double' or 'conjugal' gravestones. Just outside the main doorway there is a flat stone inscribed with the initials AW – according to local tradition, this was the grave of the first Romany to be buried in Wales.

Llangelynnin

Llanegryn

At Eglwys y Santes Fair ac Egryn Sant (Saint Mary and Saint Egryn church), which stands just above the village of Llanegryn, the fine oak rood screen dates from the 14th century and separates the nave of the church from the chancel. The roods and carvings have been lost, but the original carved panels are still intact in all their complex beauty. It is a national treasure and one of the few surviving original screens to be found anywhere in Wales. It is remarkable in having avoided interference by the notorious 'restorers' at the time of the Reformation and during the Victorian Age. Perhaps the tastes of a renowned Welsh gentry family living nearby – the Wynnes of Peniarth –

Eglwys Llanegryn

had some influence over the fate of the church. A number of memorials to the family are to be seen in the churchyard. The family at Peniarth played a vital part in the preservation of mediaeval manuscripts in *Cymraeg*, transferring them at a later date to the National Library of Wales in Aberystwyth.

Llanfihangel-y-pennant

Llanfihangel-y-pennant
In the far reaches of Dyffryn Dysynni, stands the church of Llanfihangel, nestling at the foot of the lower slopes of Cader Idris. The circular churchyard signifies the ancient nature of this devotional site. The present church dates from the 12th century and like many mediaeval churches, it has been dedicated to Mihangel (Michael). There is a leper's window on the north side. Because of the nature of that disease, the lepers were not allowed into the church itself, but they were allowed to follow the service from outside through the window provided.

Eglwys Fair (St Mary's) Tal-y-llyn
This small church stands on a hillock at the lower end of Llyn Myngul. The barrel-sided ceiling has been constructed from planks above the altar and is covered with striking paintings from the 14th century. Behind and above the door, there is an *englyn* (4-line strict metre stanza) which welcomes all those who come there in the right spirit.

Eglwys Fair, Tal-y-llyn

Aberdyfi – the meeting place of tywysogion (princes)

Afon Dyfi is one of Wales' natural boundaries with three mediaeval kingdoms conjoining on its banks – Gwynedd, Powys and Y Deheubarth. Many important declarations were made on the banks of the Dyfi which served as a convenient meeting place to discuss issues of national importance.

The village of Aberdyfi originally grew around a number of taverns and rest houses associated with the ferry that would cross the estuary in the Middle Ages. The Romans discovered copper in the hills nearby and they built a fort to control the ford in Pennal a little further upstream.

In the 6th century, Maelgwn Gwynedd summoned all the *tywysogion* throughout Wales together on the south beach at the mouth of Afon Dyfi (near Ynys-las today). His intention was to settle who should become high-king, and a competition was organised to test their courage. Each *tywysog* brought his throne along with him and, at low tide, placed it on the beach – which is still called Traeth Maelgwn. As the tide turned, it was agreed that the last one to leave his throne and flee the rising waters would be the high- king of Wales. The *tywysogion* had brought along very grand thrones which were richly adorned with precious metals and stones so that they could make an impression – all of them except Maelgwn. He sat on a seat made of goose feathers held together with wax which floated gently while all the other competitors wallowed in the rising tide. Maelgwn won easily, and henceforth it was to Gwynedd that the rest of Wales looked for leadership to preserve its independence.

Looking out towards Traeth Maelgwn

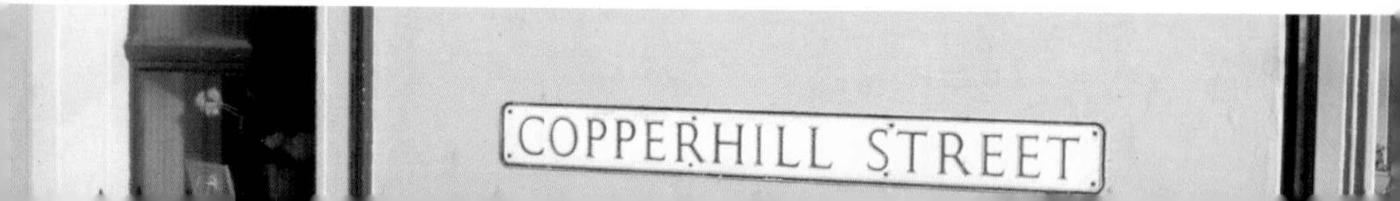

In 1140 the clerics of Wales convened in Aberdyfi and at this meeting protested against Canterbury's interference in Welsh ecclesiastical affairs. They were adamant that they had an independent church, much older than the institution in England.

In the 13th century, Llywelyn Fawr of Gwynedd became a past master at resisting the Normans who were intent on usurping and governing Wales as they pleased. They did not succeed, however, and after a lifetime of successful resistance, Llywelyn called the leaders of the *Cymry* together on the banks of Afon Dyfi, where, in 1216, the Treaty of Aberdyfi was drawn up confirming all Llywelyn's gains and proclaiming him as the overlord of Wales. Several centuries later, Aberdyfi saw magnificent ships from France, Spain and Scotland sailing in on the tide and heading up Afon Dyfi as far as Derwen-las. From there, their passengers – ambassadors and representatives of their monarchs – travelled to Machynlleth for the first meeting of the *senedd* (parliament) of the *Cymry*. The year was 1404, and Owain Glyndŵr, the father of modern Wales, had set the whole of Wales alight and was waging a war of independence. Representatives were summoned to the town on the banks of Afon Dyfi where Owain was proclaimed prince.
Over the centuries, meetings on the banks of Afon Dyfi have played a critical part in the development of modern Wales.

During the era of the independent *tywysogion,* the smallest administrative unit was the *cwmwd* (commote). *Cwmwd* Tal-y-bont contains the dyffrynnoedd of Dysynni, Mawddach and Wnion and *Cwmwd* Ystumanner consists of Tywyn, Aberdyfi and Pennal. Every *cwmwd* had its castle of earth and wood which served as an administrative centre or *maerdref*. The *maerdref* for Ystumanner was at Castell Cynfal above Rhydyronnen; the remains of the Tal-y-bont *maerdref* are at Y Domen Ddreiniog near Pont Dysynni.

Although the Normans succeeded in making a few incursions into Wales, the *Cymry* stood firm and defeated them at the battle of Coed Yspwys in 1094, driving them out of Gwynedd and the west. The *Cymry* were not conquered as the English had been. Hardly any Normans had ventured into Meirionnydd for two centuries. However, the *ardal* was a bone of contention between the *tywysogion* of Gwynedd and Powys, with both claiming it for themselves. Rhys, *tywysog* of the southern kingdom of Y Deheubarth also had to stick his oar in, building a small castle at Aberdyfi between 1151 and 1157 at Pen y Bryn (the site is now occupied by the bandstand). Llywelyn Fawr exercised a strong influence in this *ardal* in the 13th century. He was a great advocate of commerce and established a small town and market at Tywyn. Around 1221, he built a castle, originally of wood, and later of stone, at Castell y Bere on a rocky crest above Afon Dysynni. He employed 200 stone masons to undertake the work and paid them a *ceiniog* (penny) a day. The elongated D-shaped towers, which were less likely to collapse if they were undermined

Y Domen Ddreinic

The castle's locatio at Pen y Bryn, Aberdyfi

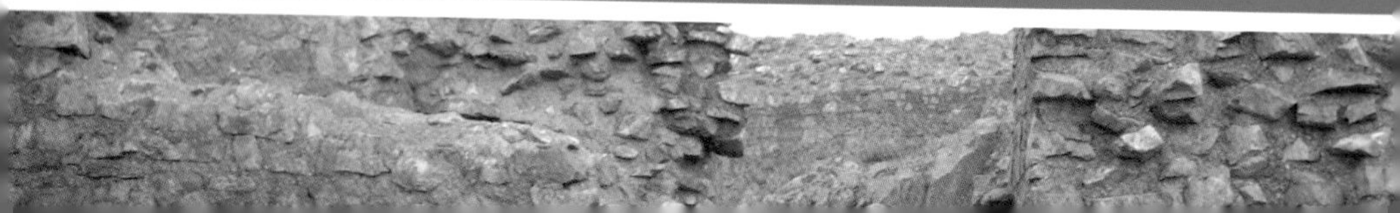

during an attack or siege than square (English) towers, were a feature of Welsh castle-building at that time.

Castell y Bere stands today in a beautiful and romantic setting, a symbol of Welsh pride. The *Cymry* preferred to utilise the rugged independence of the mountains in the defence of their country, and Castell y Bere is a classic example of this.

Castell y Bere was a military centre for Llywelyn Fawr and Llywelyn ap Gruffudd – his grandson – who continued his campaign for independence during the latter half of the 13th century. With the exception of Caernarfon and Conwy, this is the largest castle in northern Wales and although its impressive walls have long since lain in ruin, their strength and design remain a source of admiration.

Llywelyn ap Gruffudd was killed in 1282. His brother Dafydd, continued the fight with limited resources. This castle was the last stronghold to fall into Norman hands after being besieged by an army of 3,000 in 1284. Edward I stayed there during November of that year, ordering the expansion of the walls and the establishment of a borough nearby. His ambitions to colonise the *ardal* came to an abrupt end. When the *Cymry* rose up in revolt in 1294 and destroyed the castle, the English abandoned both fortress and colony.

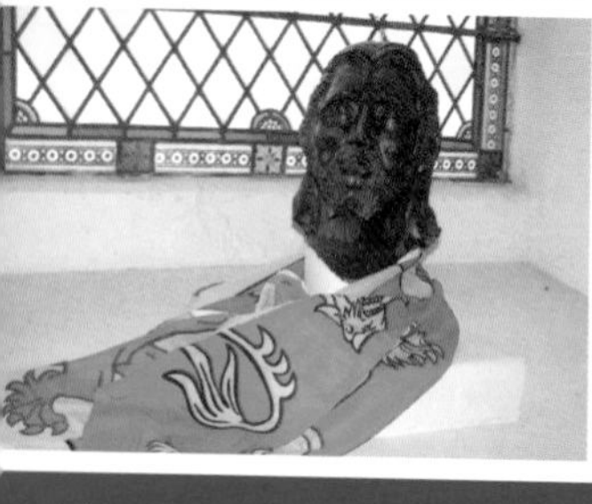

The church at Pennal was established in the 6th century by Sant Tannwg and Sant Eithrias, both Celtic missionaries from Brittany. The oval wall of the churchyard however, points to a pre-Christian sacred site. The present building exhibits many 16th century features, but some of the red stones in the wall once belonged to the nearby Roman fort.

There is a strong sense of independence to be felt at Pennal. This church served several of the Welsh *tywysogion*. During Lent 1406, Owain Glyndŵr held his final senedd in the village. *Llythyr Pennal* (the Pennal letter) is one of the most important documents in Welsh history, and is today kept in a Parisian archive. Owain Glyndŵr probably signed it in Pennal church on 31 March 1406 and sent it to Charles VI, king of France. A facsimile copy is displayed in the church.

In part of the letter, Glyndŵr outlines his programme and vision for the future of Wales – he was campaigning for the freedom of the church in Wales and for its own archbishopric at Tyddewi (St Davids), for ecclesiastical and secular officials to provide services in *Cymraeg* in Wales, for university education for Wales and for an independent government. *Llythyr Pennal* has been the political programme for Wales for centuries and by the end of the twentieth century, implementation of each and every one of its main aims had been set in motion. *Llythyr Pennal* in itself provides a sufficient reason for Owain Glyndŵr to be called the father of modern Wales.

As part of the celebrations of the 600th anniversary of Glyndŵr's rebellion in 2000,

Owain Glyndŵr's statue at the City Hall, Caerdydd (Cardiff)

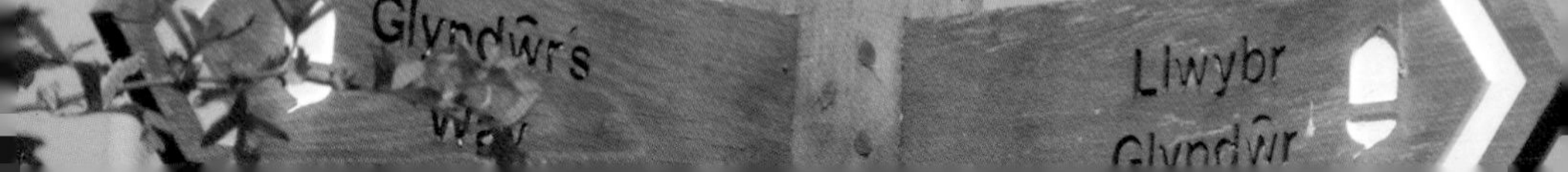

Llythyr Pennal was returned temporarily from the *Archives Nationales* in Paris to form part of a popular exhibition at the *Llyfrgell Genedlaethol* (National Library of Wales) in Aberystwyth. Here in Pennal church, there is an interpretation centre which includes a number of interesting historical items, such as the depiction by the artist, Aneurin Jones, of 'Cynulliad Cymru 1406' (the Welsh assembly 1406), a work commissioned by the church in Pennal. There is also a sculpture of Glyndŵr's head and a memorial to celebrate the establishment of *Y Cynulliad Cymreig* (The Welsh Assembly) in Caerdydd (Cardiff) in 1999.

Glyndŵr's power base was Harlech castle in north Meirionnydd and when the tides of war turned against him, he lost possession of the castle. His family were taken to the Tower of London and many of his men were killed. However, he did not give up the struggle – he went underground and continued to fight a guerrilla campaign. There is a cave which bears his name in cliffs near the mouth of Afon Dysynni. Many stories grew up about his incredible ability to strike at the enemy and escape unscathed. He was transformed from being an historical hero to becoming a mythical figure. His death went unannounced and no one knows where he is buried. His son Maredudd continued to fight as an outlaw in Meirionnydd up until 1421 and Owain came to symbolise the unyielding spirit of independent Wales.

Owain's banner

Owain's senedd-dy (parliament house) at Machynlleth

Mary Jones and her Bible

It is difficult to imagine a young girl, born in the vicinity of Llanfihangel-y-Pennant in 1784, as the inspiration for the establishment of the British and Foreign Bibles Society. That is exactly what happened, and this is her story:

Mary Jones was born at Penbryniau Mawr farm on December 16, 1784. She was christened in the parish church and the family moved to Ty'n y Ddôl.

When Mary was ten years old, a circulating school was established in Abergynolwyn by Thomas Charles y Bala. Circulating schools were a unique system in Wales whereby a teacher would teach both adults and children, focusing on reading and writing skills. This had a revolutionary effect on Welsh-speaking communities. Consequently, a much larger proportion of the peasantry in Wales were literate in their own language than in any other western European country. The result was that during the 19th century, Wales was blessed with a lively and extremely productive publishing industry. Mary learnt to read, and, every week after that, would walk two miles along mountain tracks to the farm where she could practise reading the Welsh Bible, learning many passages off by heart.

She started to save money in order to buy her own Bible. She kept hens and sold eggs; she sold honey and would knit for people. She worked and saved for six years. One tempestuous morning when she was still only 16 years old, and walking the familiar track, she met a man on a white horse. He asked her where she was going and she told him she was going to read the Bible and that she had saved her pennies to buy one in *Cymraeg* for herself. The stranger was none other than Thomas Charles (a renowned evangelist), and he

Thomas Charles' memorial in Y Bala

told her a specific time when she she should go to Y Bala because he was expecting a fresh consignment of bibles from London. When the time came, Mary had at last saved sufficient money to make her purchase. Her mother packed her some bread and cheese, together with the money and her clogs (in those days it was customary to walk barefoot in order to save wear and tear on clogs).

After a long trek over the hills to Y Bala, Mary had to face the disappointment of being told that the bibles had not yet arrived. The young girl began to cry because she had nowhere to stay, but Thomas Charles took care of her and found her somewhere to stay until the bibles were delivered. He was generous enough to give her three bibles for the price of one because she had waited so long. She was so delighted that she almost ran all the way home, (some 40km)! By 1862, Mary was a widow and blind and living on her own in a little cottage in Bryn-crug, when this story was related to a local governess in her own words. Her final resting place can be seen in the chapel cemetry in the village.

The insufficient supply of bibles in *Cymraeg* had concerned Thomas Charles for quite a while and he had made representations about this on numerous occasions. Mary's tears prompted him to make a further appeal. The authorities subsequently agreed to print more Welsh Bibles and that led to the establishment in 1804 of the British and Foreign Bible Society.

Mary Jones' grave at Bryn-crug

Bryneglwys Slates

The Industrial Revolution saw a tremendous surge of building work in the rapidly expanding towns of central and northern England. Much of this activity was dependent on raw materials from Wales. The *bro* (neighbourhood) between Dysynni and Dyfi had its own contribution to make in this construction boom. Slate was the predominant material produced in the area and there were several small quarries already at work. The remains of the largest quarry in central Wales are to be found at Bryneglwys near Abergynolwyn some seven km up the *dyffryn* from Tywyn.

The quarry was opened originally by John Pughe, a local business man from Penegoes, and in 1864, the foundation of a new company, the Aberdovey Slate Company Ltd., brought about the quarry's expansion. Local streams were used to turn water wheels providing a cheap power source for the cutting mills, and a railway to Tywyn was built to replace the old system of carrying slates on the back of mules to Pennal from where they would be transported in carts to Aberdyfi.

By 1877, the productivity of the quarries had reached its peak – a total of 8000 tonnes of slate were carved out of the mountain that year, providing work for 1,300 men.

The village of Abergynolwyn sprang up because of the quarry and its associated railway. In 1860 it consisted of just a few cottages, but then the quarry company built 70 houses in three streets. They looked like houses from industrial towns and yet, nestling in the hills as they do, they are

aesthetically very pleasing and there is plenty of space around them. The railways fulfilled two roles: as well as carrying slates down to the coast, goods could also be sent by train up the *dyffryn*. The narrow gauge line ran behind the houses so that coal could be delivered easily from house to house. To accommodate the quarrymen and their families three chapels were built as well as a church in 1879.

Bryneglwys was primarily a slate quarry and as was the case with the majority of the Welsh quarries, the quality of the craftsmanship was exceptionally high. The old craft of *hollti* (splitting) and *naddu* (dressing) is still practised at the Amgueddfa Lechi (National Slate Museum of Wales) at Llanberis – and there is no doubt that it was the craftsmanship of the quarrymen which gave Welsh slate its reputation as the best in the world.

Despite the quality of its product, the investments made in Bryneglwys eventually became too great a burden for the viability of the company. The quarry was sold twice and closed for the last time in 1946. Today, the underground passages are extremely dangerous, but there are a number of footpaths through the woods on the slopes and enough spoil heaps, remains of tramlines and disused mills to get an idea of the hive of activity that once existed here.

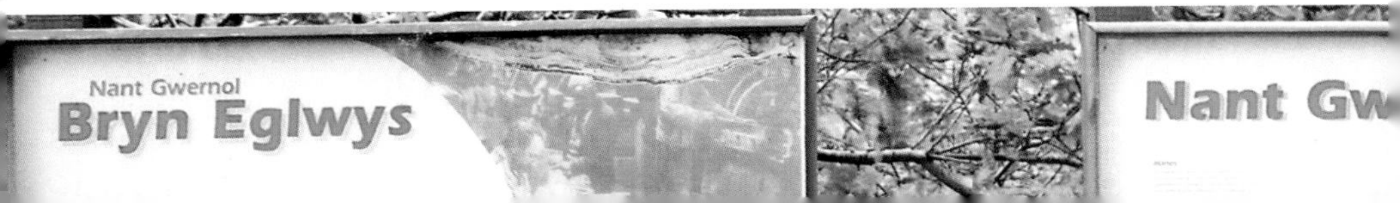

The Tal-y-llyn Narrow Gauge Railway

Whilst travelling in one of its carriages through the quiet Meirionnydd countryside, or enjoying the atmosphere of the Victorian week or the Santa Claus express at Christmas, it is easy to forget that this was at one time essentially an industrial railway line. When Bryneglwys quarry was developed, at a height of 300m above sea level, in 1864, it was on the wrong side of the mountain to take advantage of the Afon Dyfi tramway which linked Corris and Machynlleth with the harbour at Derwen-las. It was a laborious task transporting the slates on the back of mules and sledges along the rough tracks from Pennal and on to Aberdyfi. When the quarry was enlarged, a tramway was developed from Bryneglwys down to Nant Gwernol to Abergynolwyn and then a narrow gauge line running through Dôl-goch, Brynglas and Rhydyronnen to the slate quay in Tywyn. The only substantial construction work involved was the building of an impressive three-arched viaduct at Dôl-goch.

The main coast line from Aberdyfi to Llwyngwril had been opened since 1863, and thus Tywyn became a convenient depot for slate, to be reloaded onto main line trains and despatched to the English Midlands or on to sailing ships from Aberdyfi. From the outset, the Tal-y-llyn railway was designed to carry passengers as well as slates and this was the first narrow gauge railway in the world designed entirely for steam locomotives. To this day, only steam locomotives are used to pull the carriages.

When the quarry closed in 1947, the owner, Sir Henry Haydn Jones, the Member

of Parliament for Meirionnydd who lived in Tywyn, kept the line open for the community. This cost him £5 a week until his death in 1950. The Tal-y-llyn Railway Preservation Society was formed and in February 1951, the railway was transferred into its care. This was the first railway in the world to be saved and restored for the tourist industry.

The railway was extended from Abergynolwyn to Nant Gwernol during the 1970s. The appeal of the line and its little trains is now legendary. Some 30,000 passengers travel on it annually, enjoying the scenery, its gentle rhythms, getting a taste of a past age and using it as public transport to travel from one delightful station to the next.

At Cei Tywyn station, you can also visit the narrow gauge museum, which houses the best collection in the island of Britain of artefacts relating to narrow gauge railways. There are over 90 railways represented in the museum – which includes locomotives, trucks, signals, posters, lamps, tickets, signs, name plates, rails and all sorts of other treasures to excite historical railway enthusiasts. The purpose of the narrow gauge railway, of course, was to offer a cheaper form of transport, which was easier to build in rural areas where the terrain was difficult for a standard gauge line. It is not surprising therefore that Wales is world-famous for its tradition of 'great little trains'.

Dôl-goch viaduct

Aberdyfi Harbour

Aberdyfi was once famous for its fishermen, as well as its ferry. In 1649 there were severe food shortages but the fishermen of Aberdyfi managed to catch sufficient herring to feed the whole of southern Meirionnydd. There are also stories of Aberdyfi, along with other locations on the coast of Bae Ceredigion, being a favourite haunt of pirates.

Lead, silver, copper and zinc were all mined in the surrounding hills, and the harbour became an obvious outlet for exporting ore. Another export was oak for the shipbuilding industry. In 1827, a new road was cut along the coast from Tywyn to Aberdyfi and from there to Pennal and Machynlleth, and this was followed by the Cambrian Coast Railway in 1863.

Today, as you walk along the shore at Aberdyfi, it is difficult to imagine the hive of activity here when the harbour was in its heyday. Slates from Bryneglwys quarry would be brought by thelittle train to the *cei llydan* (broad quay) at Aberdyfi built by the Cambrian Company in 1882, where previously sea spray had lashed fishermen's cottages. The site of the modern-day car park was covered by a network of rails carrying trucks for loading and unloading.

Another stretch of railway was opened up to Machynlleth in 1867 and when this linked up with the Aberdyfi line, slates from the quarries at Corris and Aberllefenni, together with lead from Dylife, were brought to the harbour at the mouth of Afon Dyfi. For a while there was every possibility that Aberdyfi would develop as a port for Ireland. That never transpired, but steamers used to plough back and forth to Waterford. As recently as 1900, over 200 ships called at Aberdyfi, to unload coal and lime and collect

cargos of slate and lead.

Shipbuilding was another important industry which developed in conjunction with the harbour. A number of shipyards were built along the shore at Aberdyfi – there were seven yards at Penhelig alone. Over one hundred oak ships were built there using wood from the Dyfi forest. Local oak was particularly suitable for making masts. It is strange to think that some of these ships rounded the Horn to return with guano from Chile and Peru.

Saving lives at sea was an important concern at the little port. The first lifeboat arrived in 1837 and a new shed was erected to house it at Penhelig in 1884, the lifeboat remaining in operation until 1931. Nowadays a fast inshore rescue craft operates from the village.

With the decline in the old industries, the harbour was neglected and the winter storms left their scars. In 1965, the quay came into the care of the town council and seven years later action was taken to protect the harbour by means of an outer wall of steel around the old wooden frame. The old railway tracks were taken up and the warehouses demolished, a maritime garden, promenade and car parks being developed in their place. The words of the song, *Clychau Aberdyfi* are reflected in the logo (a black bell on a white sail) of the Dyfi Sailing Club formed in 1949.

Travellers and Visitors

When the Turnpike Trust built the road through Aberdyfi to Tywyn in 1827, the number of people travelling to the *ardal* increased, followed by a growth in the demand for the provision of new services. The Corbet family of Ynysmaengwyn, Tywyn, were a very affluent and influential family and it was they who first saw the opportunity this offered. They built the Corbet Arms Family Hotel at the west end of Aberdyfi in 1829, to provide accommodation and refreshments for those travelling by coach. It became a thriving business, in particular with the advent of the railway a decade or so later. The hotel was extensively rebuilt in 1867 but was not a great success and eventually burnt down in 1914. The Corbet Arms Hotel which the family built near the church in Tywyn was more successful and is still a thriving business.

The Tywyn Pier Company was established in 1876 and a large crowd gathered on the beach to watch the ceremonial laying of the foundations. Work was begun on the pier in 1877, but when it was only half finished, the whole structure was swept away in a dreadful storm. The waves of Cantre'r Gwaelod had triumphed again, and the whole venture was forgotten – but Ffordd y Pier still remains a street name on the foreshore!

For centuries, pilgrims would visit Ffynnon Cadfan ('Cadfan's well') in Tywyn where there was a tradition stretching back to the Middle Ages of extending hospitality to strangers. The well was enlarged into a hot and cold bath house in the 17th century, complete with showers, steam rooms and changing rooms. Droves of people travelled to Tywyn in the hope

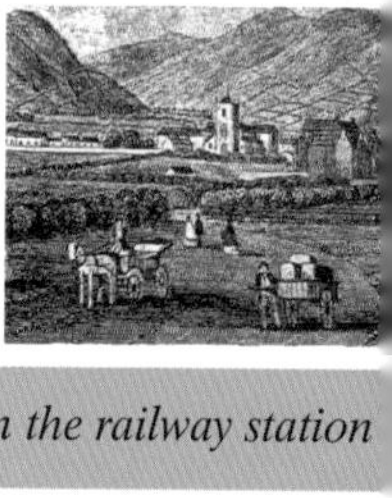

An 1869 print of Tywyn from the railway station

Penhelig

of curing arthritis, nervous disorders and gout, as well as a host of other ailments. There were croquet lawns and a lawn for playing quoits. They were very popular in the Victorian era; however by 1895, their former glory had long since faded. The baths were closed and stables built over them.

The success of Pen-y-bont hotel, built in the 16th century on the shores of Llyn Myngul at Tal-y-llyn, was more long-lasting. It was a coaching inn and walkers and fishermen began to frequent it in large numbers. There are carvings of some of the fish caught and a record of their weight at the nearby Ty'n-y-Cornel hotel.

The promenade in Tywyn was built in 1890 and still attracts summer visitors. Golf was played in Wales for the first time in Aberdyfi. The club was established in 1892 and hosted the first Wales Golfing Union Tournament in 1895. The course still ranks among the top championship courses in Wales.

The Penhelig hotel, Aberdyfi, was built by a sea captain in 1780. It has maintained its link with the sea, as those familiar with its local dishes will know. In 1904, the Trefeddian hotel was built on a hill overlooking Bae Ceredigion, and is is one of the largest hotels in this part of Wales. It has been extended and entirely refurbished, and is very popular throughout the year.

Efo Deio i Dywyn (Off with Deio to Tywyn)

There is an old folksong in *Cymraeg* which portrays a journey by two men from Llanwddyn (in Maldwyn (Montgomeryshire)), who walked all the way to the fair at Tywyn. That was quite a trek – about 42km, entirely on foot of course, stopping here and there for *bara a chaws* (bread and cheese) and *cwrw* (beer). But it must have been worth the effort because the travellers stayed at the fair for three days and wept when it was time to go home!

There were only five towns throughout the whole of the old county of Meirionnydd, and the song gives us a graphic picture of how Tywyn was once a commercial centre for much of the south of the county. The town was established by Llywelyn Fawr, its popular weekly market being held every Monday. The day of the fair, however, was a really special occasion. According to his charter, the stallholders were entitled to set up their stalls around the church of Cadfan Sant every Easter.

The custom of holding a funfair on the streets every Easter Monday has continued and it has been an important attraction for visitors on one of the first holiday weekends of the year. In those days there would be carousels, rock stalls and all sorts of bric-à-brac. In 1984, there was an experiment to extend the right to put up stalls all along Stryd Fawr rather than restricting them to one corner. It was a tremendous success and is now a permanent feature. The fair at Tywyn is still an exciting event for young and old alike.

The weekly market is held in a field on the edge of town, and this too draws the crowds. An imposing Market Hall was built in 1898 so that

Ynysmaengwyn family arms

the local farmers had somewhere under cover to sell their produce. Trade at the Hall died away in the 20th century and it was deserted for years. The building was then restored and a number of different shops were opened inside. The open-air market also flourished as small traders and local produce came into vogue once more.

A number of traditional market town crafts have been revived at Tywyn and Aberdyfi, and, by now, the *ardal* has several excellent potters who make and sell their work there. Among the other crafts you can find are basket making, glass, leather and ceramics, candles, clocks, furniture, prints, woollen goods and wrought iron, as well as crafts made of local slate.

There is a great deal of truth in the last verse of the old song, that it's worth coming to Tywyn to get a bargain:

Os bydda'i fyw un flwyddyn eto…

If I should live twelve months more
All my earnings I would store;
For the rare old pleasure when I go
Once more to Tywyn with Deio.

Some to the sea and some to the mountain

It doesn't really matter whether you prefer sea or mountain, Aberdyfi/Tywyn has plenty to offer. This combination is the essence of the Outdoor Pursuit Centre at Aberdyfi. This centre was the first of its kind, affording young people the opportunity to attend residential courses and to enjoy adventure activities on the *aber* (estuary) of Afon Dyfi and the mountains of Cader Idris. By now the idea has taken hold and has spread all over the world.

Dedicated walkers come to the *ardal* to tackle two long-distance paths and to enjoy the incredible variety of the terrain and scenery. Both paths begin or end at Aberdyfi – Llwybr Arfordir Meirionnydd (the Meirionnydd coastal path) (115km) and Llwybr Dyffryn Dyfi (the Dyffryn Dyfi path) (173km). There are plenty of other more leisurely walks for families along the coast and the floor of the *dyffrynnoedd*. One of the most accessible peaks is Craig yr Aderyn (180m) which provides a superb platform from which to look down on the splendour of Dyffryn Dysynni. This is the only place on the island of Britain where cormorants nest out of sight of the sea.

The fish in the rivers, the lakes and the sea still attract. The fishing tradition remains strong in Llyn Myngul, boats and licences being available from the Ty'n-y-cornel hotel. Even if you prefer your fish served up on a plate, there is plenty of local produce for sale from local fishermen as well as on restaurant menus.

There is nothing like water and woods to draw visitors. Apart from the lakes and the estuaries, one of the loveliest hidden haunts in the *ardal* is Ceunant Dôl-goch (Dôl-goch

gorge) about 8km from Tywyn up the *dyffryn* from Tal-y-llyn. The gorge was given as a gift to the inhabitants of the town from the landowner and recently the paths and bridges have been given a makeover. It's worth climbing over the gate and taking a stroll there. There is a series of three waterfalls, a lattice of entwined branches above the gorge, the smell of fresh moss in the air and birdsong all around. It is indeed *Tir y Tylwyth Teg* (a fairy realm).

There are nearly 10km of beautiful, clean sands on the coast, stretching from the *aber* of Afon Dysynni to the *aber* of Afon Dyfi. There are plenty of quiet spots for those who are keen to avoid the crowds. The *ardal* is also renowned for its mild, fine weather even in mid-winter. There are also plenty of entertainment facilities within reach of the more popular beaches. The paddling pool on the promenade at Tywyn is a great favourite with the younger children.

In the *canolfannau croeso* (tourist information centres) (see *www.visitsnowdonia.info*) you can get details of pony-trekking, sailing, tennis, golf, bowls, cycle hire, bird-watching as well as of hiring equipment for both wind- and wave-surfing, and opening times for the local swimming pools. In Tywyn too, you can taste the local *hufen iâ mêl* (honey ice-cream) – wonderful stuff whatever the weather!

Tywyn Leisure Centre

Oriel Llwyngwril

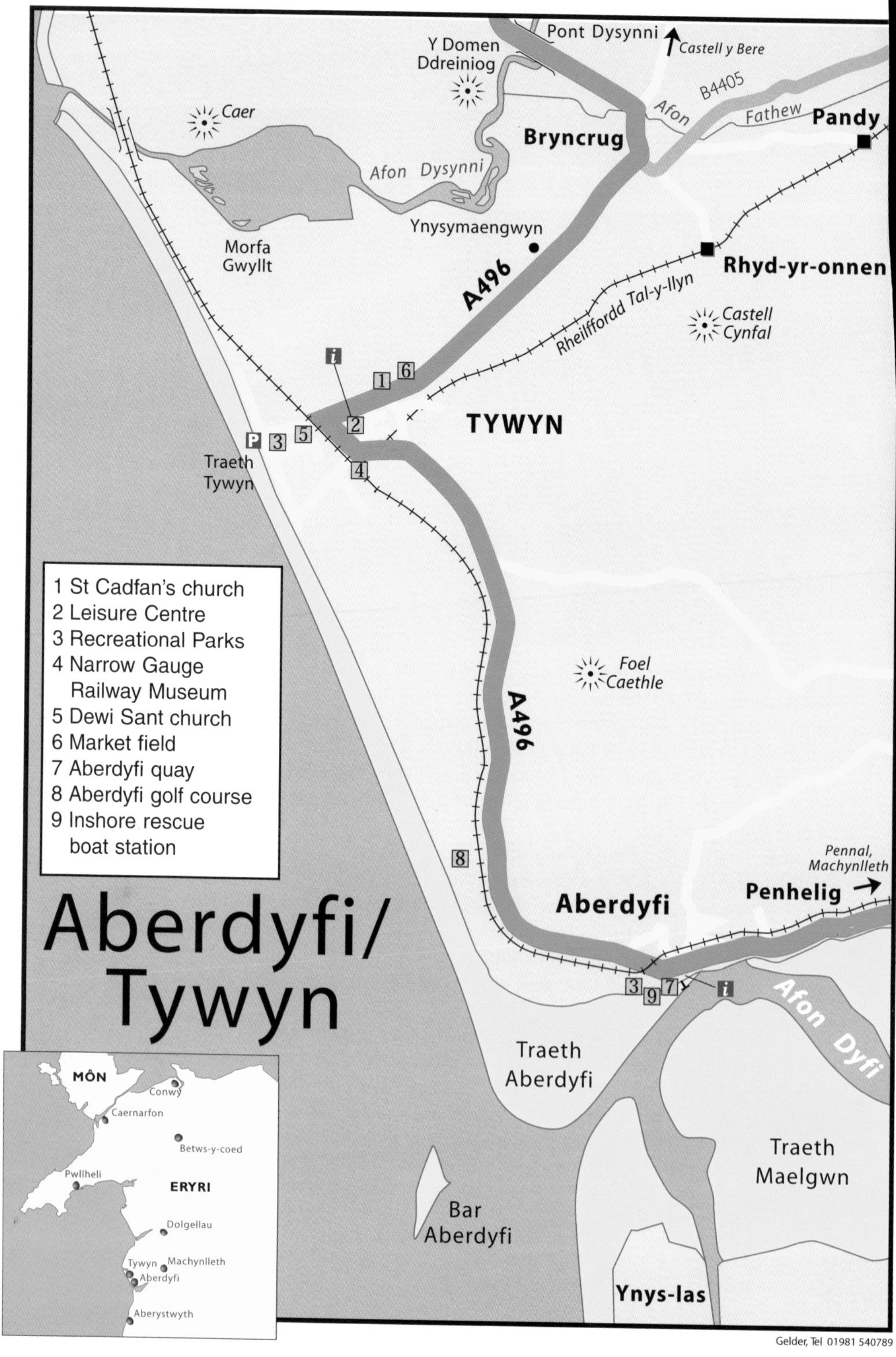

Gelder, Tel 01981 540789